World Book's Documenting History
South Africa's Anti-Apartheid Movement

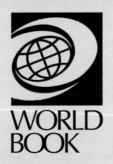

WORLD
BOOK

a Scott Fetzer company
Chicago

www.worldbookonline.com

World Book, Inc.
233 N. Michigan Avenue
Chicago, IL 60601
U.S.A.

For information about other World Book publications, visit our website at **http://www.worldbookonline.com**
or call **1-800-WORLDBK (967-5325)**.

For information about sales to schools and libraries, call **1-800-975-3250 (United States)**, or **1-800-837-5365 (Canada)**.

Library of Congress Cataloging-in-Publication Data

South Africa's anti-apartheid movement.
  p. cm. -- (World Book's documenting history)
  Includes bibliographical references and index.
  Summary: "A history of the anti-apartheid movement in South Africa, based on primary source documents and other historical artifacts. Features include period art works and photographs; excerpts from literary works, letters, speeches, broadcasts, and diaries; summary boxes; a timeline; maps; and a list of additional resources" -- Provided by publisher.
  ISBN 978-0-7166-1507-1
  1. Anti-apartheid movements--South Africa--History--Juvenile literature. 2. Apartheid--South Africa--History--Juvenile literature. 3. South Africa--Race relations--History--Juvenile literature. 4. Anti-apartheid movements--South Africa--History--Sources--Juvenile literature. 5. Apartheid--South Africa--History--Sources--Juvenile literature. 6. South Africa--Race relations--History--Sources--Juvenile literature. I. World Book, Inc.
  DT1757.S68 2011
  323.168--dc22

                    2010017507

World Book's Documenting History
Set ISBN 978-0-7166-1498-2
Printed in Malaysia by TWP Sdn Bhd, JohorBahru
2nd printing January 2012

Staff

Executive Committee

President
  Donald D. Keller
Vice President and Editor in Chief
  Paul A. Kobasa
Vice President Marketing/Digital Products
  Sean Klunder
Vice President, Licensing & Business Development
  Richard Flower
Controller
  Yan Chen
Director, Human Resources
  Bev Ecker

Editorial

Associate Director, Supplementary Publications
  Scott Thomas
Editor
  Sara Dreyfuss
Senior Editor, Supplementary Publications
  Kristina Vaicikonis

Manager, Contracts & Compliance
(Rights & Permissions)
  Loranne K. Shields
Researcher, Supplementary Publications
  Annie Brodsky
Editorial Researcher
  Jon Wills
Administrative Assistant
  Ethel Matthews

Editorial Administration

Director, Systems and Projects
  Tony Tills
Senior Manager, Publishing Operations
  Timothy Falk
Associate Manager, Publishing Operations
  Audrey Casey

Manufacturing/Production/Graphics and Design

Director
  Carma Fazio
Manufacturing Manager
  Steven K. Hueppchen
Production/Technology Manager
  Anne Fritzinger
Production Specialist
  Curley Hunter
Proofreader
  Emilie Schrage
Manager, Graphics and Design
  Tom Evans
Coordinator, Design Development and Production
  Brenda B. Tropinski
Senior Designer
  Isaiah W. Sheppard, Jr.
Associate Designer
  Matt Carrington

Marketing

Associate Director, School and Library Marketing
  Jennifer Parello

Produced for World Book by
Arcturus Publishing Limited

Writer: Cath Senker
Editors: Patience Coster, Alex Woolf
Designer: Jane Hawkins

Contents

South Africa Colonized

MANY AFRICAN PEOPLES, INCLUDING HUNTER-GATHERERS AND FARMERS, lived in South Africa before the arrival of Europeans. In 1652, Dutch farmers established a colony in the Cape of Good Hope in South Africa. The settlers became known as Boers, and later Afrikaners. In 1795, Britain (later also called the United Kingdom) captured the Cape. British settlers began to arrive in South Africa, too. The Europeans had superior weapons to the Africans. The Europeans fought to take over the Africans' land and other resources. The British and Boers also came into conflict. They fought two major wars. The Boers won the first, in 1880 and 1881. The British defeated the Boers in the second war, from 1899 to 1902.

◀ An 1872 woodcut of diamond mining in Colesberg, now in Northern Cape province, South Africa. In 1867, diamonds were discovered along the Orange River near Hopetown. In the 1870's, prospectors found gold in the Transvaal (now mostly Gauteng, Mpumalanga, and Limpopo provinces). The desire for South Africa's riches caused conflict between the Boers and British.

▶ Thomas Phipson (1815-1876), the sheriff of Natal (now KwaZulu-Natal) in the mid-1800's, complains in a letter about the local Xhosa people. He calls them Kaffirs, which is now considered an offensive term. Phipson describes the Africans as lazy and morally inferior to Europeans. Such beliefs helped the Europeans justify a policy of *segregation* (separation by race). The South African poet Ralph N. Currey (1907-2001), Phipson's great-grandson, collected the sheriff's writings in a book published in 1968.

Creatures, however, having fewer legs than insects, and commonly called Kaffirs, are practically the greatest hindrances [blocks] to successful agriculture in Natal. [They are] crafty and cunning, at once indolent [lazy] and excitable . . . debased and sensual to the last degree.

Thomas Phipson, mid-1800's

▲ Boers fight from a trench in Transvaal during the Anglo-Boer War of 1899-1902. Most of the Boers (now called Afrikaners) were farmers of Dutch ancestry. They established two independent republics, the Transvaal in 1852 and the Orange Free State (now Free State) in 1854. The British and Boers fought two wars. After the British won the war of 1899-1902, the two Boer republics became British colonies.

▶ Martin Lutuli (mid-1800's-1921), a Zulu chief, speaks to a South African government panel in 1904 about his people's hopes for equality. The panel, the South African Native Affairs Commission, interviewed many people of European and African descent about relations between the races in South Africa. The commission's report, published in 1905, formed much of the basis for the government's official policy of segregation. Lutuli was the former chairman of an African group called the Natal Native Congress.

Sometimes we discuss about how we should approach the Government to let the Native have the franchise, so that the Native can have a voice in the Parliament. . . . We also want to approach the Government to let the Natives be free in everything, let them buy lands if they like, if they are able to, and let them trade in the towns . . . . We also talk about education; we say we have not got enough education.

Martin Lutuli, May 28, 1904

NOW YOU KNOW

- Beginning in the 1600's, Europeans settled in South Africa.
- The Boers and the British fought for control of the country and its resources.
- African people wanted equality with white people.

The Union of South Africa

IN 1910, CAPE COLONY, NATAL, THE TRANSVAAL, AND THE ORANGE FREE STATE joined to form the Union of South Africa. The United Kingdom allowed the new country to rule itself as part of the British Empire. South Africa's Constitution gave whites almost total power. The British and Afrikaners (people of mostly Dutch, German, or French ancestry) shared control in the new government. The Natives' Land Act of 1913 set aside about 7 percent of South Africa's land for black people, who made up about 80 percent of the population. White people could settle in the remaining area, which included the main towns and the regions with rich resources.

1

As against the European the native stands as an eight year old against a man of mature experience—a child in religion, a child in moral conviction; without art and without science; with the most primitive needs and the most elementary knowledge to meet these needs. . . . When he achieves his majority in development and civilization, and stands on an equal level with the white man, his adulthood will be acknowledged.

J. B. M. Hertzog, early 1900's

◀ The Boer leader James Barry Munnik Hertzog (1866-1942), usually called J. B. M. Hertzog, argues in a speech that blacks are too childlike to govern themselves. Today, his opinions would be considered racist. Hertzog founded the National Party in 1914 to promote the interests of the Boers. He served as South Africa's prime minister from 1924 to 1939.

2

▶ The Union Buildings, which house the nation's government, stand at the highest point in Pretoria, capital of the new Union of South Africa. Sir Herbert Baker (1862-1946), a British architect, designed the buildings in the Neoclassical style, resembling the architecture of ancient Greece. They were completed in 1913.

3

Some readers may perhaps think that I have taken the Colonial Parliament rather severely to task. But... if you see your countrymen and countrywomen driven from home, their homes broken up, with no hopes of *redress* [correction of the injustice], on the *mandate* [order] of a Government to which they had loyally paid taxation without representation [in Parliament]—driven from their homes, because they do not want to become servants... you would, I think, likewise find it very difficult to maintain a level head or wield a *temperate* [moderate] pen.

Sol T. Plaatje, 1916

◀ Sol T. Plaatje (1876-1932), a Tswana writer and political leader, describes the suffering created by the Natives' Land Act of 1913 in his book *Native Life in South Africa*. Plaatje was a founding member of the South African Native National Congress (SANNC). Black South Africans formed the SANNC, a forerunner of the African National Congress (ANC), in 1912 to fight for justice for black people.

4

▶ Sol Plaatje (seated, far right) and the other members of an SANNC delegation pose together in 1914. The delegation went to the United Kingdom in June of that year to protest the Natives' Land Act and to ask the British government to help them. However, the British government did not want to offend the Afrikaners and offered no assistance.

NOW YOU KNOW

- The Union of South Africa set aside most of the land for the white population.
- Many Europeans argued that African peoples were unable to rule the country.
- Black South Africans formed the SANNC to fight for black rights.

Afrikaners on the Rise

FROM THE 1920's TO THE 1940's, AFRIKANERS ACHIEVED MANY OF THEIR GOALS. Their language, Afrikaans, became an official language of South Africa along with English. Most Afrikaners farmed for a living, and many were poor. The government created jobs in cities to help poor Afrikaners but did not offer the same opportunities to black South Africans. Black workers got only a fraction of the wages paid to whites. In 1923, the SANNC shortened its name to the African National Congress (ANC). The ANC became the main political voice for blacks. In 1931, South Africa gained full independence as a member of the Commonwealth of Nations, an association of the United Kingdom and some of its former colonies.

▶ The African Bill of Rights calls for citizenship rights for people of African descent. In 1923, the South African Native National Congress (SANNC) held its annual convention in Bloemfontein, South Africa. There, the SANNC changed its name to the African National Congress (ANC) and adopted the African Bill of Rights. The document argues that Africans should have the same rights as Europeans, including the right to vote.

1

That the peoples of African descent have, as an integral and inseparable element in the population of the great Dominion of South Africa, and as undisputed contributors to the growth and development of the country, the constitutional right of an equal share in the management and direction of affairs of this land of their permanent *abode* [home], and to direct representation by members of their own race in all legislative bodies of the land....

Article V of the African Bill of Rights, 1923

2

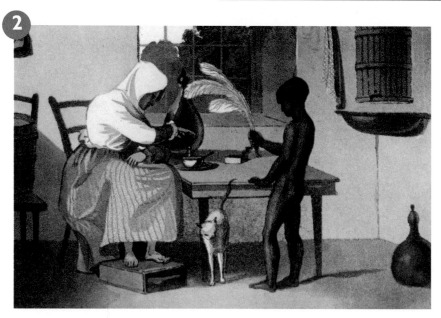

◀ A 1931 illustration shows an Afrikaner woman working in her kitchen, assisted by a young black servant. Poverty forced many black girls and boys to become servants or farmworkers at a young age.

4

He [the Afrikaner] was looked down upon, he had to come with his hat in hand, he had to be satisfied with the crumbs which fell from the tables of the rich. To make any sort of progress . . . he had to beg the English oppressor and had to obey his every command. Any job that was offered him, however humiliating, dangerous and lowly paid it might have been, he had to accept with gratitude. He and his family had to be satisfied with the worst living conditions in dirty ghettoes.

Kerk en Stad (Church and City) 1947

◀ *Kerk en Stad (Church and City)*, a study ordered by the Dutch Reformed Church of South Africa in 1947, describes conditions among Afrikaners. The study portrays Afrikaners as underdogs in white South African society. The Dutch Reformed Church was a mostly Afrikaner church and was naturally sympathetic to its own members.

3

▶ A South African miner bakes bread in an oven in the outdoor kitchen of the workers' quarters at a diamond mine in Kimberley, South Africa, in 1930. Black mineworkers were paid a fraction of the wages earned by their white counterparts for similar work. Mine owners also required laborers to live close to the mine where they worked.

NOW YOU KNOW

- From the 1920's and to the 1940's, Afrikaners achieved many of their goals. Afrikaans became an official language along with English.

- The government introduced measures to raise the living standards of Afrikaners.

- The African National Congress (ANC) argued that black people should have equal rights.

Fighting for Change

DURING THE 1940'S, RESENTMENT OF WHITE RULE GREW among black South Africans. Many of them believed that World War II (1939-1945) had been fought for democracy. They also saw many Asian and African countries gain independence from their colonial rulers. Blacks started to take action. The African National Congress set up the ANC Youth League for young people in 1944. Nelson Mandela (1918-) was a founding member. The Communist Party of South Africa (now the South African Communist Party), founded in 1921, also became more active. The ANC and the Communist Party supported a miners' strike in 1946. The police crushed the strike, but it inspired resistance to white rule.

▶ These passages from the *ANC Youth League Basic Policy Document* support African nationalism—the belief that Africa should be ruled by people of African descent. Nationalism was growing in strength across the continent. The Youth League issued the document in 1948.

1

The African people in South Africa are oppressed as a group with a particular colour. They suffer national oppression in common with thousands and millions of oppressed Colonial peoples in other parts of the world....

The African has a primary, inherent and *inalienable* [unable to be taken away] right to Africa which is his continent and Motherland, and the Africans as a whole have a divine destiny which is to make Africa free among the peoples and nations of the earth.

In order to achieve Africa's freedom the Africans must build a powerful national liberation movement... and it should be led by the Africans themselves.

ANC Youth League Basic Policy Document, 1948

2

◀ People in Alexandra township, a black living area in Johannesburg, bicycle past an empty bus during a 1957 bus boycott. The residents of Alexandra refused to use the buses in protest of high fares. Boycotts in 1943, 1944, and 1957 succeeded in forcing the bus company to reduce fares.

3

[The] Gold Mining Industry considers that trade-unionism as practised by Europeans is still beyond the understanding of the tribal Native.... A *trade union* [labor union] organisation... would not only be useless, but *detrimental* [damaging] to the ordinary mine Native in his present stage of development.

Chamber of Mines, 1946

◀ The Chamber of Mines, an organization of mine owners, argues that blacks should not have the right to form unions. This argument reflects the common belief among white people that people of African descent were backward and inferior to Europeans. Although unions of black workers were illegal, South African gold miners staged widespread strikes in 1946.

▼ South African police attack striking mineworkers in Witwatersrand in August 1946. At that time, white mineworkers earned 12 times as much as black workers. The black miners went on strike to demand higher wages. The police crushed the strike after about a week.

4

NOW YOU KNOW

- Black resentment of the government grew in the 1940's, influenced by the independence movements in other African countries.
- Nelson Mandela was a founding member of the ANC Youth League in 1944.
- Bus boycotts and strikes aimed to improve the conditions of black people.

Apartheid Becomes Law

THE NATIONAL PARTY WON THE 1948 ELECTION. Its leader, Daniel François (D. F.) Malan (1874-1959), became prime minister. Malan believed in the superiority of Afrikaners. Under his leadership, the National Party began to set up South Africa's system of *apartheid* (rigid separation by race). The main apartheid laws were the Prohibition of Mixed Marriages Act of 1949, which banned marriages between races; the Population Registration Act of 1950, which classified people by race; and the Group Areas Act of 1950, which created separate residential areas for the races. The Suppression of Communism Act of 1950 banned Communism. The government labeled anyone who opposed apartheid as a Communist.

▶ G. Eloff, an Afrikaner scientist who studied heredity, justifies apartheid in religious terms in *Rasse en Rasvermenging (Races and Race Mixing),* 1942. Many Afrikaners believed that God had chosen them as a special race. It was a Christian duty to keep their people pure and to avoid mixing with other races.

1

The preservation of the pure race tradition of the *Boerevolk* [Afrikaner people] must be protected at all costs in all possible ways as a holy pledge entrusted to us by our ancestors as part of God's plan with our People. Any movement, school, or individual who sins against this must be dealt with as a racial criminal by the effective authorities.

G. Eloff, 1942

▼A road sign in Johannesburg warns motorists to be on their guard for native (black) pedestrians. During the apartheid era, many signs in public places, such as beaches and parks, indicated whether whites or nonwhites could use the facilities.

2

3

A White person is one who is in appearance obviously white—and not generally accepted as Coloured—or who is generally accepted as White—and is not obviously Non-White, provided that a person shall not be classified as a White person if one of his natural parents has been classified as a Coloured person or a Bantu....

A Bantu is a person who is, or is generally accepted as, a member of any aboriginal race or tribe of Africa....

A Coloured is a person who is not a White person or a Bantu.

Population Registration Act of 1950

◀ The Population Registration Act of 1950 gives definitions of the various races who lived in South Africa. The act divided people into four categories: (1) White, (2) Asian, (3) Coloured (mixed race), and (4) Bantu (black). To be classified as white, a person had to look white and have parents who were classified as white.

4

▶ South African police line up against protesters opposing apartheid laws in Cape Town in June 1950. Passage of the Group Areas Act and the Suppression of Communism Act triggered the demonstration. About 500 black and European demonstrators marched to Parliament. The police attacked the crowd with batons and injured a number of people.

NOW YOU KNOW

- The National Party won the election in 1948 and introduced the system of apartheid.
- Apartheid laws classified people by race and separated the races.
- Many South Africans opposed apartheid from the beginning.

Living Under Apartheid

THE APARTHEID LAWS HAD WIDE-RANGING EFFECTS. They forced the four defined racial groups—white, Asian, Coloured (mixed race), and African (black)—to live in separate areas. Many families had to split up because some family members were classified as a different race from the others. The inequality between black and white living standards grew. Most facilities for nonwhites, such as hospitals, transportation, and schools, were inferior to those for whites. Only white people had access to high-level jobs with good salaries. The Asians, most of whom were people of Indian ancestry, and the Coloureds suffered under apartheid, too.

▲ A black servant walks with well-dressed white children in Cape Town. The sign declares that this area is for "white persons only." In the cities, white people typically lived in large homes and had black servants. Household workers, such as housemaids and gardeners, could enter white areas only to do their job.

2

It has been estimated that if the zoning plans of the Durban City Council are fully implemented 35 Indian schools with an enrolment of 8,771 pupils will be uprooted. This will have [a] devastating effect on Indian education in Durban....

Thousands of Indian businesses in Durban will be ruined as a result of the proclamation....

Not only are businesses and homes affected but also mosques, temples and churches, notwithstanding the fact that Moslems and Hindus regard their places of worship as *sacrosanct* [not to be treated with disrespect]....

The proclamation of June 6th has the immediate effect of making large areas owned and occupied by our people in and around Durban immediate Group Areas for white ownership.

Natal Indian Congress, 1958

◀ A report by the Natal Indian Congress describes the harmful effects of the Group Areas Act of 1950 on Asian Indians. The Indian leader Mohandas K. Gandhi (1869-1948) had founded the congress in 1894 to fight discrimination against Asian Indians.

▶ Former residents of Sophiatown, South Africa, tell a journalist about being forced to move from their homes. Sophiatown was a mixed community of black, Coloured, and Asian families in Johannesburg. In 1955, the government evacuated Sophiatown to make way for a new white suburb.

3

"It was very difficult for me to lose a house which I was born in," says Patricia Mokoena-Harvey.... "Children were screaming and crying. They didn't understand what was happening—and it was very cold and raining. It was very traumatic."

"Because of the government's racial classifications and strict separation of group areas, many families were split up," says former resident Paul Mashinini. "Some members would be classified as coloured, others as black. Therefore they would be forced to live in separate townships."

from "Sophiatown: Recalling the Loss" (2005) by Lucky Sindane

NOW YOU KNOW

- Apartheid increased the inequality between black and white living standards.
- The Coloured and Asian Indian communities suffered under the apartheid laws.
- The people of Sophiatown were forced to move to make way for a white suburb.

Segregation in Education

HENDRIK VERWOERD (1901-1966) served as minister for native affairs from 1950 to 1958 and as prime minister of South Africa from 1958 to 1966. Verwoerd saw the education system as the key to creating a segregated society. The Bantu Education Act of 1953 brought most educational institutions under government control. The law enforced apartheid by separating black and white students. The government spent far less money on black students than on white ones. In 1959, despite opposition from students and teachers, the Extension of University Education Act stopped white universities from accepting black students.

▶ Hendrik Verwoerd, then minister for native affairs, explains his education policy in a 1954 speech to Parliament. Verwoerd states that black children should be educated only to serve their own community and to work for white people as laborers. They should not be allowed to mix with Europeans or to hold professional jobs. Verwoerd thus concludes that there is no point in offering black students a high level of education.

1

There is no space for him [i.e., the Bantu] in the European community above certain forms of labour . . . . it is of no avail for him to receive training which has its aim in the absorption of the European community, where he cannot be absorbed. Until now he has been subjected to a school system which drew him away from his community and misled him by showing him the greener pastures of European society in which he was not allowed to graze.

Hendrik Verwoerd, 1954

2

Our history, as we had absorbed it from the tales and talk of our elders, bore no resemblance to South African history as it has been written by European scholars, or as it is taught in South African schools, and as it was taught to us at Fort Hare. The European insisted that we accept his version of the past and what is more, if we wanted to get ahead educationally, even to pass examinations in the subject as he presents it. . . . we studied this history not merely in the white man's version . . . but in a distinctly pro-Boer version.

from *Freedom for My People* (1981) by Zachariah K. Matthews

◀ Zachariah K. Matthews (1901-1968), a South African lawyer, expresses frustration with the education he received in the 1920's. He attended the University College of Fort Hare, now the University of Fort Hare. In the 1920's, it was the only South African university to accept nonwhite students.

3

▲ A teacher gives a lesson in a segregated classroom in the Crossroads settlement, a mostly black residential area on the outskirts of Cape Town. The government required schools to teach the white version of history and other subjects. The curriculum stressed that whites were superior to blacks and that South Africa belonged to the Afrikaners.

NOW YOU KNOW

- In the 1950's, the South African government separated the education systems for black and white students.
- Government leaders believed that black children should be educated mainly to become laborers serving the white community.
- Black students learned the white version of history.

The Defiance Campaign

AFTER 1948, GROWING NUMBERS OF SOUTH AFRICANS JOINED THE CAMPAIGN to resist apartheid. In 1949, the ANC announced an aggressive policy called the Programme of Action. It encouraged strikes, boycotts, and civil disobedience—the deliberate, public refusal to obey apartheid laws. In 1952, the ANC and an organization of Asians called the South African Indian Congress launched the Defiance Campaign Against Unjust Laws. The Defiance Campaign was a mass movement to disobey apartheid laws. For example, black protesters walked into whites-only areas, stayed out after curfew, or burned their pass books, the identity papers that every black person had to carry. Thousands of people were arrested.

1

It should be understood clearly that the Government will under no circumstances entertain the idea of administrative or executive or legislative powers over Europeans, or within a European community, to Bantu men and women, or to other smaller Non-European groups. The Government therefore, has no intention of repealing the long existing laws differentiating between European and Bantu.

Prime Minister D. F. Malan's
private secretary, 1952

◀ The private secretary of Prime Minister D. F. Malan responds by letter to a request from the African National Congress (ANC) that South Africa do away with unjust apartheid laws. The secretary writes that the government has "no intention" of allowing nonwhite people any power over Europeans.

2

▶ Supporters of the Defiance Campaign Against Unjust Laws gather in Fordsburg, a suburb of Johannesburg, on April 6, 1952. Speakers at the meeting included James S. Moroka (1891-1985) of the ANC and Yusuf M. Dadoo (1909-1983) of the South African Communist Party.

3

I started following up the papers, and read about the people defying here and there. And then one day I went down to the Orlando plantation [a mostly black residential area in Johannesburg] and saw the cars coming to pick up the people to defy, so calm and brave. And I asked myself, "What is this great thing?" So I went back home and told my mother that I wanted to defy. My daughter was very ill in hospital, under tubes, and my mother did not like the idea of my leaving my daughter. So that night I took her up to the top of the hill and showed her all the lights of Orlando. I said, "Should I serve all these lights, or serve my daughter? This defiance is for the people; my daughter is mine alone." And my mother said I must defy.

Lilian Ngoyi, undated

▲ The anti-apartheid leader Lilian Ngoyi (1911-1980) relates how and why she joined the Campaign of Defiance even though she was a widow with two children and an elderly mother to support. The campaign was South Africa's first large-scale movement to oppose apartheid. More than 8,000 volunteers went to jail for defying apartheid laws. They were jailed for failing to carry passes, for violating the curfew on blacks, and for entering facilities reserved for whites.

4

► Nelson Mandela stands in the office of Mandela and Tambo, a law firm he founded with Oliver Tambo (1917-1993) in Johannesburg in 1952. It was the first black law partnership in South Africa. Mandela and Tambo provided low-cost legal aid to black people and defended those accused of violating apartheid laws.

NOW YOU KNOW

- The Defiance Campaign Against Unjust Laws began in 1952.
- The campaign gave black people the courage to stand up to white people.
- Nelson Mandela and Oliver Tambo set up the first black law firm in South Africa.

Protesting for Freedom

IN 1955, THE ANC FORMED A BROAD ALLIANCE WITH SEVERAL GROUPS, including the South African Indian Congress, the South African Coloured People's Organisation, and the South African Congress of Trade Unions. The groups gathered over 3,000 delegates for a Congress of the People in Kliptown, near Johannesburg, on June 25-26, 1955. The congress adopted the Freedom Charter, a statement calling for racial equality, liberty, and human rights. The government reacted by arresting 156 leaders on charges of treason, including Nelson Mandela, Oliver Tambo, and Walter Sisulu (1912-2003). Their trial lasted from 1956 until 1961.

1

We, the people of South Africa, declare for all our country and the world to know:

That South Africa belongs to all who live in it, black and white, and that no government can justly claim authority unless it is based on the will of all the people…

That only a democratic state, based on the will of all the people, can secure to all their birthright without distinction of colour, race, sex or belief…

The Freedom Charter, June 26, 1955

◄ The opening words of the Freedom Charter set forth several basic principles of democracy. These principles include the idea that government derives its authority to govern from the will of the people. The opening of the charter also states that all people have equal rights, regardless of their color, race, gender, or religion.

2

► Delegates at the Congress of the People read the Freedom Charter section by section in three languages—English, isiXhosa, and Sesotho. The government claimed that the charter was a Communist document. Communism was illegal under the 1950 Suppression of Communism Act.

3

TREASON TRIAL

he
USED

DECEM
195

The anti-apartheid leaders accused of treason pose for a group photograph in December 1956. Charges against 61 of the accused were later dropped. Nelson Mandela, *circled,* is standing in the third row, near the middle.

4

On all the evidence presented to this court and on our finding of fact it is impossible for this court to come to the conclusion that the African National Congress had acquired or adopted a policy to overthrow the state by violence.... The accused are accordingly found not guilty and are discharged.

Justice F. L. H. Rumpff,
March 29, 1961

▲ The judge's verdict in the Treason Trial in 1961 finds the defendants not guilty of treason. The prosecution tried to show that the Freedom Charter was a Communist document that could only be achieved by overthrowing the South African government. The judge agreed with the prosecution that the ANC had been working to replace the government with a different kind of state. He also admitted that the ANC had used illegal forms of protest. But he said that the prosecution failed to prove that the ANC was using violence to overthrow the government and that its actions did not amount to treason.

NOW YOU KNOW

- In 1955, an alliance of anti-apartheid organizations adopted the Freedom Charter.
- In 1956, the government arrested 156 leaders of the movement and charged them with treason.
- In 1961, after a long trial, the judge declared the defendants not guilty.

Repression and Resistance

THE GOVERNMENT TRIED TO CONTROL THE RESISTANCE TO APARTHEID by enacting many laws starting in the mid-1950's. Law enforcement officers gained wide-ranging powers to arrest people, ban organizations, and stop meetings. The pass laws, which required black men over the age of 16 to carry identity papers, were extended to nonwhite women in 1956. The Publications and Entertainment Act of 1963 allowed the government to ban works it believed "undesirable." As a result, the government could censor the information that the public received.

▲ A policeman checks the pass book of a South African man. Blacks had to carry identity papers with details of their work history whenever they entered white areas. The pass laws enabled the government to control the movement and employment of nonwhites.

▼ The anti-apartheid leader Albertina Sisulu (1918-   ) describes taking part in the Women's March on Pretoria. On Aug. 9, 1956, some 20,000 women marched to the Union Buildings in the capital to protest the pass laws. Sisulu was a founding member of the Federation of South African Women, a multiracial body established in 1954 to oppose apartheid. Large numbers of women, most of them nonwhite, joined the movement during the 1950's.

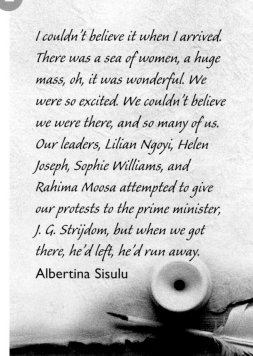

I couldn't believe it when I arrived. There was a sea of women, a huge mass, oh, it was wonderful. We were so excited. We couldn't believe we were there, and so many of us. Our leaders, Lilian Ngoyi, Helen Joseph, Sophie Williams, and Rahima Moosa attempted to give our protests to the prime minister, J. G. Strijdom, but when we got there, he'd left, he'd run away.
Albertina Sisulu

3

◀ Protesters carry stacks of petitions to the Union Buildings, South Africa's capitol, during the 1956 Women's March on Pretoria. The petitions, with thousands of signatures, call for the end of the pass laws. The women left the petitions at the prime minister's office door.

4

▶ A South African journalist, not named, describes how the prime minister of the Transkei threatened to ban his newspaper and arrest him. The Transkei (now part of Eastern Cape province) was an area that the South African government reserved for the Xhosa people during the period of apartheid. Government pressure led many newspapers to censor themselves and avoid publishing articles critical of the government.

We were kept under very tight control because (the newspaper management) were afraid of being banned. They knew how sensitive a lot of issues were. A significant amount of the stuff I wrote was spiked [not published] and most of the rest of it was doctored [changed]. Matanzima [Prime Minister George Matanzima of Transkei] knew that the Daily Dispatch was afraid of being banned and this had the effect of self-censorship on the newspaper. Every day in Parliament, George Matanzima would say: "The Daily Dispatch reporter sitting up there writing nonsense about us —we will ban the newspaper, we will detain you."

Unnamed journalist, 1980

NOW YOU KNOW

- In the 1950's, the government passed many laws to try to halt the opposition to apartheid.
- In 1956, the government extended to nonwhite women the pass laws, which required people to carry identity papers.
- The government used censorship to try to stop the spread of anti-apartheid views.

The Movement Splits

IN THE LATE 1950's, THE FAILURE TO ACHIEVE CHANGE caused frustration and division within the anti-apartheid movement. Some ANC leaders, such as Nelson Mandela and Albert Luthuli (1898-1967), continued to work with organizations of different racial groups. These organizations included the Congress of Democrats, which had mainly white members. Other ANC members, led by Robert Mangaliso Sobukwe (1924-1978), wanted white people to have no role in their movement. They desired a purely African movement. Sobukwe left the ANC and founded the Pan Africanist Congress (PAC), becoming its first president in 1959.

1

We the black people
Are crying out for our land
Which was taken by crooks.
They should leave it alone.

Anthem of the Pan
Africanist Congress, 1960

◄ The anthem of the Pan Africanist Congress (PAC) accuses white people of stealing black people's land. PAC leaders split from the ANC in part because they rejected the ANC's multiracial policies. They thought the ANC had grown too close to white organizations, such as the Congress of Democrats and the South African Communist Party. The founders of the PAC believed that whites could not be trusted because they benefited from the apartheid system.

2

► Nelson Mandela explains in his 1994 book *Long Walk to Freedom* his view of why the PAC broke away from the ANC. Mandela and other ANC leaders disagreed with the PAC's view that blacks should keep themselves separate. Instead, the ANC believed that all races should work together to achieve a unified South Africa.

The PAC echoed the axioms [principles] and slogans of that time: Africa for the Africans and a United States of Africa. But the immediate cause for their breakaway was their objection to the Freedom Charter and the presence of whites and Indians in the Congress Alliance leadership. They were opposed to interracial cooperation, in large part because they believed that white communists and Indians had come to dominate the ANC.

Nelson Mandela, 1994

3

▲ The PAC *insignia* (symbol) is black, green, and gold. Black stands for Africa's people, green for its fertile land, and gold for its mineral wealth. The symbol shows the African continent with a star over Ghana, the first European colony in Africa to gain self-government. The PAC hoped to rename South Africa "Azania" once the country came under black rule. South Africa outlawed the PAC in 1960 but legalized it again in 1990. It is now a small political party called the Pan Africanist Congress of Azania.

NOW YOU KNOW

- In 1959, the anti-apartheid movement split, and the Pan Africanist Congress (PAC) was formed.
- The PAC wanted a purely black anti-apartheid movement.
- The ANC believed that all racial groups should struggle together against apartheid.

The Sharpeville Massacre

IN 1960, THE PAC AND THE ANC ORGANIZED PROTESTS AGAINST THE PASS LAWS. Black South Africans left their pass books at home, went to police stations, and gave themselves up. In Sharpeville, now part of Vereeniging, thousands of people surrounded the police station on March 21. The police opened fire and killed 69 black demonstrators in what became known as the Sharpeville Massacre. The shooting set off strikes and marches throughout the country. Opposition to apartheid also came from outside South Africa. Many leaders of the Commonwealth of Nations criticized South Africa's policies. In 1961, South Africa became a republic and left the Commonwealth.

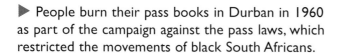

▶ People burn their pass books in Durban in 1960 as part of the campaign against the pass laws, which restricted the movements of black South Africans.

▼ The bodies of the dead and injured lie on the ground after the massacre at Sharpeville on March 21, 1960. When South Africans learned about the shooting, anger erupted against the government.

3

▶ A story about the Sharpeville Massacre appears in the British newspaper *The Guardian* on the day after the shootings. The story reports 63 rather than 69 killings.

The first African was shot dead and four Africans and several policemen were injured after the police had been stoned. The Africans retaliated [fought back], causing casualties among the police. The police then opened fire with sub-machine guns, Sten guns [light submachine guns], and rifles, and eye-witnesses said that the front ranks of the crowd fell like ninepins [bowling pins]. The crowd then retreated, leaving their dead and wounded in the street.

Mangled bodies of men, women and children lay sprawled on the roadway of the square. One policeman described the scene as "like a world war battlefield."

The Guardian, March 22, 1960

4

At the meeting I argued that the state had given us no alternative to violence. I said it was wrong and immoral to subject our people to armed attacks by the state without offering them some kind of alternative. I mentioned again that people on their own had taken up arms. Violence would begin whether we initiated it or not. Would it not be better to guide this violence ourselves, according to principles where we save lives by attacking symbols of oppression, and not people? If we did not take the lead now, I said, we would soon be latecomers and followers to a movement we did not control.

Nelson Mandela, 1994

◀ Nelson Mandela explains in *Long Walk to Freedom* how he persuaded the ANC to adopt a policy of armed struggle after the Sharpeville Massacre. He delivered these arguments at a meeting in June 1961 of the ANC National Executive Committee, which made most major decisions for the organization. At the meeting, the committee decided to change the ANC's strategy to one of violent resistance.

NOW YOU KNOW

- The PAC and the ANC organized protests against the pass laws in 1960.
- The police shot 69 people dead during a demonstration in Sharpeville.
- After the Sharpeville Massacre, the ANC agreed to begin violent resistance to apartheid.

After Sharpeville: Sabotage

After the Sharpeville Massacre, the ANC formed a military wing called Umkhonto we Sizwe ("Spear of the Nation"). Umkhonto we Sizwe launched a campaign of sabotage. It bombed government buildings, power stations, and transportation facilities. The PAC started a similar military wing called Poqo. The South African government passed the General Law Amendment Act (or the Sabotage Act) of 1962 to strengthen the powers of the police. By the end of 1964, the government had succeeded in stopping the sabotage.

◀ A tower that supported electric power lines lies crumpled after a bombing in December 1961 by Umkhonto we Sizwe and another group, the National Committee for Liberation, later the African Resistance Movement (ARM). Umkhonto we Sizwe set off bombs that month at electric power stations and government offices in Johannesburg, Port Elizabeth, and Durban.

The time comes in the life of any nation when there remain only two choices: submit or fight. That time has now come to South Africa....

We of Umkhonto have always sought—as the liberation movement has sought—to achieve liberation without bloodshed and civil clash. We do so still. We hope, even at this late hour, that our first actions will awaken everyone to a realisation of the disastrous situation to which the Nationalist [National Party] policy is leading.

Manifesto of Umkhonto we Sizwe,
Dec. 16, 1961

▶ Umkhonto we Sizwe states its aims in a public declaration called a manifesto. It says that the group hopes to achieve freedom by peaceful means but will fight if necessary. Umkhonto we Sizwe distributed thousands of leaflets with this manifesto.

3

▲ Police and crime scene investigators examine the evidence after a bomb explosion at a Johannesburg railway station on July 24, 1964. Umkhonto we Sizwe and the PAC militant group Poqo ("Blacks Only," later the Azanian People's Liberation Army) carried out dozens of bomb attacks in the early 1960's.

▶ The Sabotage Act of 1962 lists a wide range of activities that were classified as sabotage. The government passed the act to crack down on the bomb attacks. The law provided for sabotage to be punished with the same penalties as treason—including death.

4

... any person who committed any wrongful and wilful act whereby he/she injured, obstructed, tampered with or destroyed the health or safety of the public, the maintenance of law and order, the supply of water, light, power, fuel or foodstuffs, sanitary, medical or fire extinguishing services could be tried for sabotage.

Sabotage Act of 1962

NOW YOU KNOW

- The ANC and the PAC launched a campaign of bombings and other sabotage in 1961 to try to force the government to change its policies.
- The government passed the Sabotage Act of 1962 to help combat the sabotage campaign.
- By the end of 1964, the government had stopped the sabotage.

ANC Leaders in Prison

IN 1963 AND 1964, THE GOVERNMENT ARRESTED NELSON MANDELA, Walter Sisulu, Jacob Zuma (1942-   ), and other ANC leaders. Mandela, Sisulu, and Zuma were sentenced to life imprisonment for sabotage and conspiracy. Robert Sobukwe of the PAC also got a life sentence. The leaders were sent to a harsh prison camp on Robben Island, near Cape Town, to do manual labor. The ANC moved to the African country of Zambia. Although support for the ANC grew abroad, the South African government continued its apartheid policies and tightened security. Most of the white population supported the government's position against the ANC.

1

◀ Supporters of Hendrik Verwoerd, prime minister of South Africa from 1958 to 1966, carry a huge poster of his likeness on a march in Bloemfontein in 1961. The words "Ons vir jou Suid-Afrika" on the banner mean "O South Africa, dear land." Verwoerd, called the "architect of apartheid," shaped apartheid first as minister of native affairs and then as prime minister.

2

▶ Christo Brand (1960?-   ), a prison guard on Robben Island, recalls starting to keep watch over the ANC prisoners in 1978. He says that the prisoners seemed less dangerous than he was told. Brand befriended Nelson Mandela in prison and taught him to speak Afrikaans. Brand discussed his time working on Robben Island in a 1999 interview with a British journalist on the TV series "Frontline."

. . . the head of the prison . . . explained that we worked with the biggest criminals in history in South Africa. . . . the first day, they took me first to the sergeant in charge, introduced me to him [Mandela]. Then the opposite cell from the office was a chap, Andrew Mlangeni, he came in and he said, "Oh, a new warder [guard]," and he asked my surname in Afrikaans. He had totally a different approach [than] the head of the prison told us. This man was speaking Afrikaans fluently and you couldn't see he was dangerous.

Christo Brand, 1999

3

▶ Nelson Mandela (left) talks with Walter Sisulu in the prison yard at Robben Island in 1966. The prisoners spent most of the time working or locked in tiny cells. They were permitted to exercise or relax in the yard only for short periods.

4

For more than five years we have been forced to do heavy and uncreative work which sapped our energy and in some cases even adversely [badly] affected our health. Through this period you condemned us to a monotonous routine of either breaking stones, doing pick and shovel work, and denied us all opportunities for any kind of vocational training, or of any work that may encourage and develop a sense of self-respect, industry and responsibility in the prisoner, and no efforts are being made to help us to lead respectable and meaningful lives when released.

Nelson Mandela, 1970

◀ Mandela complains to the head of the South African prison system about the hard labor prisoners were forced to do on Robben Island. He wrote this letter of complaint to General J. C. Steyn, the commissioner of prisons, in January 1970. Mandela became a spokesman for the political prisoners—people imprisoned for opposing the government.

NOW YOU KNOW

- In 1964, Nelson Mandela and other ANC leaders were sent to prison on Robben Island.
- The conditions in prison were tough.
- Mandela became a spokesman for the political prisoners.

The Bantustans

To SEPARATE BLACKS FROM WHITES, the South African government set aside 10 areas for blacks called bantustans or homelands. Some were the traditional homes of a particular ethnic group. Others were settled only after the government forced people to move there. Blacks were no longer citizens of South Africa. Four homelands—Bophuthatswana, Ciskei, Transkei, and Venda—became independent in name only. The other six had limited self-rule. All 10 had little real power. The bantustans had poor soil and no industry, so most residents had to travel to the cities to make a living. Most black South Africans opposed the homeland system.

It is accepted Government policy that the Bantu are only temporarily resident in the European areas of the Republic for as long as they offer their labour there. As soon as they become, for one reason or another, no longer fit for work or *superfluous* [no longer needed] in the labour market, they are expected to return to their country of origin or the territory of the national unit where they fit ethnically if they were not born and bred in their homeland.

Government circular about the homeland policy, 1967

◄ A 1967 circular from the Department of Bantu Administration and Development explains that all blacks must move to bantustans unless white employers need them as laborers. The government viewed black labor as a resource for the convenience of the white population. The "European areas" of South Africa were all the regions that were not homelands.

► A Mfengu woman describes how she was forced to move in 1977. The South African government made the Mfengu leave their homes in Tsitsikama, Eastern Cape, and relocate to Elukhanyweni in Ciskei. The government then sold their land to white farmers. It claimed that blacks moved to the homelands voluntarily, but the testimony of many people contradicted that claim.

When they came to us, they came with guns and police. . . . They did not say anything, they just threw our belongings in [the government trucks]. . . . We did not know, we still do not know this place. . . . And when we came here, they dumped our things, just dumped our things so that we are still here. What can we do now, we can do nothing. We can do nothing. What can we do?

Unnamed Mfengu woman, 1983

3

▲ Police force residents of Sophiatown, a Johannesburg township, from their homes and load their belongings onto trucks. Apartheid restricted blacks to living in townships, separate areas on the outskirts of cities. The government evacuated and bulldozed many townships to build new housing for whites.

NOW YOU KNOW

- The government forced the different African peoples to move to 10 separate areas known as homelands or bantustans.
- South Africa gave the homelands limited powers of self-government.
- The economies of the bantustans were poor, so many blacks still had to go to the cities to find work.

Township Resistance

THE GOVERNMENT MOVED SO MANY BLACKS TO THE HOMELANDS that those regions became overcrowded. During the 1960's and 1970's, many black South Africans resisted the homeland policy and moved to towns and cities. The Coloured (mixed race) and Asian population in urban areas increased, too. Apartheid laws restricted nonwhite people to living in separate areas called townships, many of them far from the city center. Although the government tried to divide the townships into separate areas for what it called the African "tribes," different races and ethnic groups mingled together. Most people in the townships lived in poverty. Residents built their own shacks. Few homes had electric power or running water.

1

This way I salute you:

My hand pulses to my back trousers pocket

Or into my inner jacket pocket

For my pass, my life,

Jo'burg City.

My hand like a starved snake rears my pockets

For my thin, ever lean wallet,

While my stomach groans a friendly smile to hunger,

Jo'burg City.

   "City Johannesburg" (1972) by Mongane Wally Serote

◄ The South African poet Mongane Wally Serote (1944-   ) writes about the poverty in Soweto. In the 1970's, Soweto was a separate township for black South Africans in the city of Johannesburg. The phrase "thin, ever lean wallet" refers to his lack of money.

2

► Alex La Guma (1925-1985), a Coloured writer and political leader, describes the growing alliance against apartheid in his 1972 paper "Apartheid and the Coloured People of South Africa." La Guma was a founder of the South African Coloured People's Organisation (SACPO). During the 1960's and early 1970's, people from the Coloured and Indian communities joined the black campaign for freedom.

In a very real sense, the future of the Indian and Coloured people and their liberation as oppressed groups is seen as being intimately bound up with the liberation of the Africans. Coloured and Indian people are increasingly seeing their liberation as an integral part of the liberation movement.
Alex La Guma, 1972

3

▲ A boy walks past houses made mainly of corrugated iron and scrap materials in Cape Town in 1979. Many South Africans lived in such shantytowns—crowded, unplanned neighborhoods of ramshackle houses. So many people moved to urban areas that it was impossible for the government to stop or control the building of shantytowns.

NOW YOU KNOW

- In the 1960's and 1970's, large numbers of Africans, Coloured people, and Asian Indians moved to separate living areas called townships on the outskirts of white cities.
- Within the townships, people of many races and ethnic groups mingled.
- Coloured and Asian Indian people in South Africa joined the campaign for black freedom.

Pressure on South Africa

I N THE 1960's AND 1970's, SOUTH AFRICA GREW INCREASINGLY ISOLATED in the world community. The southern African states of Botswana, Lesotho, Swaziland, Angola, and Mozambique gained independence from their colonial rulers. These countries began to support the anti-apartheid movement. They were too weak, however, to force change. Many stronger countries also opposed apartheid. In 1962, the United Nations General Assembly urged its members to break diplomatic and economic ties with South Africa until apartheid was ended. But many countries, including the United Kingdom, kept close economic ties with South Africa.

◀ Angolans celebrate winning their independence from Portugal in November 1975. Portugal had fought a costly war in Angola before granting the African country its freedom. South Africa supported Portugal in its struggle against the Angolan rebels. The South African government saw the spread of self-rule in African countries as a threat and tried to stop it.

▶ Peter J. McGregor (1947-2008), an organizer of the Australian Anti-Apartheid Movement, explains how the movement sabotaged sporting events to put pressure on South Africa to end apartheid.

It was clear . . . that targeting South African sport could be a means by which white South Africans could be made aware of political repression as well as human rights' violations going on in their country. . . . We started to explore whether we would engage in violence against property. A good example was at the Australian swimming championships [when] Meredith Burgmann [an Australian political leader born in 1947] and others threw dye into the pool, making it opaque [not clear]. Sabotage. It stopped the swimming carnival.
Peter J. McGregor, 1993

3

◀ In 1970, the Stop the Tour campaign demonstrates outside Lords Cricket Ground in London. The campaign kept South African rugby and cricket teams from touring the United Kingdom in 1969 and 1970. The world governing bodies of many sports expelled South Africa because of its apartheid policy. In 1964, the International Olympic Committee banned South Africa from the Olympic Games.

4

▶ A statement adopted by a conference of leading African American organizations in 1976 calls for companies to stop investing in South Africa. The Congressional Black Caucus, a group of African American members of the United States Congress, convened the conference in Washington, D.C., in September 1976.

We condemn the role played by the United States and other foreign corporations and banks, which by their presence and activities collectively have participated in the oppression of Blacks and have *undergirded* [lent support to] the repressive white minority governments of Southern Africa. No longer must Mr. Vorster [Prime Minister Balthazar Johannes Vorster (1915-1983)] be able to exact U.S. political support as ransom for America's hostage private corporations. Multinational corporations must recognise that the South African economy is not sound, and that the investment climate there is no longer favorable.

African-American Manifesto on Southern Africa, 1976

NOW YOU KNOW

- Several southern African countries gained independence in the 1960's and 1970's and supported the anti-apartheid movement in South Africa.
- There were international efforts to ban South Africa from sporting events because of its apartheid policy.
- Many African American leaders called for companies to stop investing in South Africa.

The Soweto Uprising

IN THE 1970's, PRESSURE ON THE SOUTH AFRICAN GOVERNMENT INCREASED. Young people joined the Black Consciousness Movement, which promoted self-respect among blacks. In 1976, thousands of schoolchildren march in Soweto, a black area of Johannesburg, to protest the use of Afrikaans in the schools. The police opened fire, killing two children. After the Soweto Uprising, South Africa repealed or relaxed some apartheid laws. P.W. Botha (1916-2006) became prime minister in 1978. His government allowed black workers to form unions, ended the pass laws, and lifted restrictions on multiracial sports. But whites remained in control.

1

Black consciousness is in essence the realisation by the black man of the need to rally together with his brothers … and to operate as a group in order to rid themselves of the *shackles* [chains] that bind them to perpetual servitude. It seeks to demonstrate the lie that black is an *aberration* [variation] from the "normal" which is white.… It seeks to infuse the black community with a new-found pride in themselves, their efforts, their value systems, their culture, their religion, and their outlook to life.

Steve Biko, 1978

◀ Steve Biko (1946-1977), a South African medical student, explains in *I Write What I Like* (published in 1978, after his death) the goals of the Black Consciousness Movement. It tried to raise pride in black culture. Because of Biko's popularity, the police saw him as a threat. They arrested him in August 1977. He died of injuries suffered in police custody in September 1977.

2

▶ Two months after Steve Biko's death, *Drum* magazine put a photograph of him on its cover and ran a major story about his life and his ideas. *Drum* was the most widely read magazine in Africa.

3 . . . the violence began when the police tried to . . . stop the march. The students taunted them, and they responded with teargas . . . apparently no order from the police to the marchers to disperse was heard, and a senior police officer admitted at the time that no warning shots had been fired either. The first child to be killed was evidently a thirteen-year-old schoolboy called Hector Petersen. He was killed ... apparently by a bullet fired directly at him from behind. Several other youngsters were also shot dead. Then, in the words of one newspaper, "All hell broke loose."

John Kane-Berman, 1976

▲ John Kane-Berman (1946-   ), a journalist for the South African newspaper the *Financial Mail,* describes the Soweto Uprising in June 1976. Thousands of schoolchildren marched carrying signs with such slogans as "If we must do Afrikaans, Vorster must do Zulu." Vorster refers to Prime Minister Balthazar Johannes Vorster. The uprising was triggered by a government requirement that half of all school subjects be taught in Afrikaans—the language of the whites who controlled the government. Few blacks knew the language.

▼ A father carries his son who was killed during the Soweto Uprising on June 16, 1976. In the following months, clashes between blacks and the police broke out in many areas of South Africa. Hundreds of people were killed—mostly young, black South Africans.

4

NOW YOU KNOW

- The Black Consciousness Movement encouraged blacks to take pride in their culture.
- A new rule requiring that South African school lessons be taught in Afrikaans sparked the Soweto Uprising.
- Over the following few months, hundreds of people died in riots and other disturbances.

Whites Against Apartheid

WHITE PEOPLE ALSO CAMPAIGNED AGAINST APARTHEID. Many South African church leaders criticized it. Several women's groups and organizations of university students campaigned against the government. The students at English-speaking universities, especially the universities of Cape Town and the Witwatersrand, organized political discussions and demonstrations. The Black Sash, a white women's group, supported black South Africans. The members wore black sashes as a sign of protest. Some novelists, including Alan Paton (1903-1988) and Nadine Gordimer (1923-), criticized South African racism in their work.

▶ Trevor Huddleston (1913-1998) explains in *Father Huddleston's Picture Book* (1990) why he joined the anti-apartheid movement. Huddleston, an English-born Anglican priest who moved to South Africa in 1943, opposed apartheid as a religious duty, a struggle of good against evil. In the 1950's, he served as a priest in Sophiatown, a multiracial community in Johannesburg. When the South African government forced Sophiatown's residents to leave, he and other anti-apartheid leaders organized a resistance movement.

1

I believed most strongly that fighting apartheid was a moral battle against something profoundly evil. It didn't come to me through academic reading or study. It came to me through seeing apartheid in its impact on the people who I had responsibility for as a priest...

I came back to Sophiatown at a particularly critical time when the government was determined to remove all "black spots" (as they called them) from white areas and they picked on my parish.... We knew we had to take action and we formed a protest group.

Trevor Huddleston, 1990

2

The poverty of the Africans was a wheel to which they were tied; turn, and it will run its weight over them again. . . . And if you cut them free of the wheel, that will be the end of white civilization, said some. . . . Anyway, white civilization is doomed, said others.

Nadine Gordimer, 1953

◀ In her first novel, *The Lying Days* (1953), the South African author Nadine Gordimer explains how "white civilization" was built upon the *exploitation* (ruthless use) of black South Africans and their continuing poverty. Gordimer won the 1991 Nobel Prize in literature, becoming the first South African to receive the award.

3

▲ Members of the Black Sash organization demonstrate against apartheid outside Johannesburg City Hall in 1955. The women wear black sashes as a symbol of protest against injustice.

NOW YOU KNOW

- Many South African churches criticized apartheid.
- University students and women's organizations campaigned against the apartheid government.
- Novelists criticized South African racism in their work.

Unions Gain Power

I N THE 1970'S AND 1980'S, SOUTH AFRICA'S ECONOMY BEGAN TO SUFFER because of apartheid. Many countries expressed opposition to apartheid by reducing economic ties with South Africa. Some corporations ended or limited their business in South Africa. The high cost of enforcing the apartheid laws added to the country's economic problems. Union action added to the pressures on the economy. Black labor unions became legal in 1979. The unions grew and became more powerful, especially mineworkers' unions. Mining—the digging of diamonds, gold, coal, and other minerals—formed the foundation of South Africa's economy.

1

> The presence of so many blacks together with their ever greater political, economic and social bargaining power, coupled with the perpetual interference from the outside, means that we are approaching a catastrophe, even if we eliminate *discrimination* [treating certain groups of people unfairly].
>
> Afrikaner Broederbond, 1975

◀ The Afrikaner Broederbond warns its members in 1975 of what it sees as the dangerous growth in the power of the black population. The Broederbond was a group that worked to promote the interests of Afrikaans-speaking whites. "Interference from the outside" refers to the opposition to apartheid around the world.

2

▶ The symbol of the Congress of South African Trade Unions (COSATU) depicts three black workers, one turning a wheel, one carrying a hammer, and one waving a red pennant. The slogan "An Injury to One Is an Injury to All" originated in the United States labor movement in the early 1900's. COSATU is a federation of unions founded in 1985 to coordinate the actions of black South African workers.

3

▶ A South African mineworker quotes the Hindu proverb "It takes a thorn to remove a thorn." The saying has a meaning similar to "Fight fire with fire"—that is, you should use the same methods as your opponent in a struggle. The mineworker suggests that if mine owners use force, miners will use force to combat them.

He makes us work in the factories for nothing and our children are crying. He exploits us. We workers are united. We shall fight the exploiter. It takes a thorn to remove a thorn.

Unnamed South African mineworker, 1980's

4

◀ Miners protest in 1986 after a fire in the Kinross gold mine in Eastern Transvaal killed 177 miners. The National Union of Mineworkers accused the mine owners of ignoring the safety of their employees. The union, which represented mostly black miners, became one of the largest and most powerful unions in South Africa.

NOW YOU KNOW

- During the 1970's and 1980's, South Africa's economy began to suffer as a result of apartheid.
- Many countries reduced their economic ties with South Africa.
- Unions representing black workers grew and became more powerful.

A Nation in Protest

IN 1983, SEVERAL HUNDRED ANTI-APARTHEID GROUPS FORMED A BROAD ALLIANCE called the United Democratic Front (UDF). Protests erupted all over South Africa, including boycotts, demonstrations, and *sabotage* (intentional damage to property). In 1984, the government tried to split the movement by introducing a new constitution. It gave some rights to Coloured and Asian people but none to blacks. The nonwhite communities remained united in opposing apartheid. The government declared a nationwide state of emergency in 1986, giving the police and the military sweeping powers. They could arrest and hold people without charging them.

◄ A young black man rides a bus restricted to whites in Durban in 1986. One tool of resistance was to defy the apartheid rules. Black South Africans used facilities reserved for whites, violated curfews, and refused to carry passes.

► The United Democratic Front (UDF) explains its goals in a statement from 1987. The UDF became one of the most important anti-apartheid organizations of the 1980's. It united a wide range of workers, students, and church groups of all races.

Now our broad aim is to unite the broadest mass of the people, black and white, in an unstoppable tide towards liberation. Millions of people are yearning for a new South Africa. The UDF has to organise these forces in the most effective way, so that our people can act as one, while the regime itself is divided and isolated from the overwhelming majority of the people.

United Democratic Front, 1987

3

◀ Marchers wear stickers proclaiming "UDF Lives! Forward to People's Power." The UDF launched its People's Power campaign in October 1985. The campaign aimed for residents of the townships—urban living areas reserved for nonwhites—to take over running their communities from the national government. Ordinary people began to govern the townships for themselves. They organized education, law enforcement, and even garbage collection.

▶ An article in *Fortune* magazine describes the international reaction to South Africa's declaration of a state of emergency. The state of emergency suspended many civil rights and gave the police and the military broad powers to put down protests and unrest. The police arrested thousands of anti-apartheid activists, including many UDF leaders and union members.

4

The state of emergency that a defiant President Pieter W. Botha declared in South Africa inspired near-unanimous criticism abroad—and redoubled pressure for economic sanctions against Pretoria. Botha had acted, in the face of almost certain international *censure* [criticism], because racial violence was mounting daily, and more seemed inevitable on the tenth anniversary of the Soweto uprising of June 16, 1976.

Fortune magazine, 1986

NOW YOU KNOW

• The United Democratic Front (UDF), an alliance of anti-apartheid groups, formed in 1983.

• The government declared a state of emergency to try to control the anti-apartheid movement.

• The residents of some townships began to run their own communities, taking over from the national government.

Sanctions and War

By 1986, THE UNITED STATES, EUROPEAN NATIONS, AND MANY OTHER COUNTRIES had imposed economic *sanctions* (penalties) on South Africa. To put pressure on the government to end apartheid, many countries refused to trade with South Africa or to invest money there. Meanwhile, South Africa carried out military operations against Angola to try to stop its support for the anti-apartheid movement. The Soviet Union backed Angola. South Africa claimed the attacks on Angola were necessary to defend itself from Communist influence.

1

◀ Miriam Makeba (1932-2008), an internationally acclaimed South African singer, performs at a concert in London in June 1988. The anti-apartheid movement organized the concert as a tribute to Nelson Mandela on his 70th birthday. South Africa banned Makeba in 1960 because of her anti-apartheid activities. She lived in exile in many countries from the 1960's to the 1990's, when Nelson Mandela persuaded her to return to South Africa.

2

The boycott supporters believe that nothing is to be lost by applying the pressure. It is the only effective way of forcing Pretoria [the South African government] to change course, they declare. If it means that the blacks will be hurt it is unfortunate but necessary.... The bishop [Desmond Tutu] is not convinced that the blacks would be the ones to suffer in the event of sanctions. As he once put it: "When the ladder is falling over, surely it's those at the top who will get hurt most, not those at the bottom?"

Graham Leach, 1986

▶ In *South Africa: No Easy Path to Peace* (1986), Graham Leach, a British journalist, quotes Archbishop Desmond Tutu (1931-). Tutu did not believe that black South Africans would suffer more than whites from economic sanctions. Tutu, who was the first black Anglican archbishop of Cape Town, won the 1984 Nobel Peace Prize for his anti-apartheid efforts.

3

◀ At an anti-apartheid demonstration in Boston in 1986, protesters call for "death to apartheid" and the release of Nelson Mandela. Protesters in the United States urged American universities and corporations to divest—that is, to sell off their investments in all companies doing business with South Africa.

▶ A 1985 report in *The Washington Post* indicates that the war in Angola had become a large-scale struggle. South Africa maintained that if the Soviet-allied forces won in Angola, other African countries would fall to Communism.

4

Trees have been smashed by heavy vehicles and stripped by shells, and there were hundreds of foxholes, slit trenches and underground *bunkers* [shelters], making the scene *reminiscent of* [similar to] a World War I battlefield. The earth was scarred with shell craters and scorched areas where explosions started bush fires. It obviously was a major *conventional* [regular] battle in what until now has been a *guerrilla war* [warfare conducted by roving bands of fighters who stage ambushes, sudden raids, and other small-scale attacks].

The Washington Post, 1985

NOW YOU KNOW

- Many countries used economic *sanctions* (penalties) to pressure South Africa to end apartheid.

- Protesters urged U.S. universities and corporations to sell off investments connected to South Africa.

- South Africa attacked Angola to try to stop Angolan support for the anti-apartheid movement, claiming that military action was necessary to prevent the spread of Communism.

Apartheid in Crisis

URING THE LATE 1980's, DEEP SPLITS OPENED IN SOUTH AFRICAN SOCIETY. Some whites wanted to preserve apartheid. But many Afrikaner leaders realized that apartheid could not continue in the same form and sought a way to end the crisis. Despite the state of emergency declared in 1986, anti-apartheid protests continued. Conflict also broke out within the black community. A bitter rivalry developed between the African National Congress (ANC), which had many Xhosa members, and the Inkatha Freedom Party (IFP), which was mostly Zulu. The conflict led to much violence.

◀ Sister Bernard Ncube (1932?-   ), a Roman Catholic nun and anti-apartheid leader, speaks in the 1980's. She was the first president of the Federation of Transvaal Women, founded in 1984. The group worked to protect the interests of rural women. It helped organize protests about rent increases and boycotts to support strikes. Sister Bernard was one of several religious figures who led anti-apartheid efforts in the 1980's. Others included Desmond Tutu, the Anglican archbishop of Cape Town, and Allan A. Boesak (1945-   ), a minister in the Dutch Reformed Mission Church and president of the World Alliance of Reformed Churches.

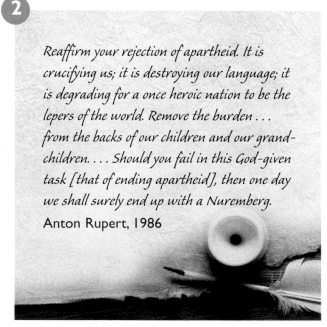

Reaffirm your rejection of apartheid. It is crucifying us; it is destroying our language; it is degrading for a once heroic nation to be the lepers of the world. Remove the burden . . . from the backs of our children and our grand-children. . . . Should you fail in this God-given task [that of ending apartheid], then one day we shall surely end up with a Nuremberg.
Anton Rupert, 1986

▶ Anton Rupert (1916-2006), a wealthy Afrikaner business leader, urges President P. W. Botha to end apartheid in a private letter in January 1986. Rupert warns of "a Nuremberg," referring to the Nuremberg Trials of Nazi war criminals from 1945 to 1949, after World War II. The economic and political crisis in South Africa in the late 1980's led Rupert and other influential white people to call for change.

3

The great division in black politics in South Africa is the division between those who support violence as the only effective means of bringing about radical change and those who reject violence because they see it as the most ineffective means of bringing about radical change.

Inkatha Freedom Party, about 1987

◀ A pamphlet published by the Inkatha Freedom Party (IFP) in about 1987 describes the gulf that had opened within the anti-apartheid movement. The Zulu leader Mangosuthu Buthelezi (1928-) had set up the IFP in 1975. It opposed the ANC's tactics of violence against the South African government. The IFP called instead for talks with the apartheid regime.

4

▶ An angry crowd at a funeral in 1985 threatens to "necklace" a man suspected of passing information to the police. Some black South Africans used "necklacing" to punish people whom they suspected of betraying the anti-apartheid movement. The "necklacers" filled a tire with gasoline, placed it around the neck of a suspect, and set it on fire. A clergyman at the funeral saved this man from death.

NOW YOU KNOW

- By the late 1980's, many Afrikaner leaders realized that they needed to change the apartheid system.
- Church leaders took on important roles in the anti-apartheid movement.
- The anti-apartheid movement was divided, especially between supporters of the ANC and supporters of the Inkatha Freedom Party.

Free Nelson Mandela!

BY THE LATE 1980's, THERE WAS WIDESPREAD SUPPORT FOR THE ANC and increasing pressure on the South African government to release Nelson Mandela. He had become an international symbol of the fight for justice. In 1989, Frederik Willem de Klerk (1936-) replaced P. W. Botha as leader of the National Party and president of South Africa. In 1990, de Klerk ended the bans on the ANC, the Pan Africanist Congress, and the South African Communist Party. On Feb. 11, 1990, Mandela walked free after 27 years in prison.

▶ Desmond Tutu describes his reaction to hearing on Feb. 10, 1990, that Nelson Mandela would be released from prison. Tutu's recollection, reported in a television interview, appears in *The Rainbow People of God* (1994), a collection of his sermons, speeches, and writings.

▼ Photographers surround ANC leader Nelson Mandela shortly after his release from prison in 1990. While in prison, Mandela had become a symbol of the struggle for racial justice. His release was a sign of the ending of apartheid.

1

It is saying to us, God hears . . . God acts, God is really involved. We've been praying so long and it seemed like our prayers were just going into a void. Now [what we prayed for] is happening. . . . We are all going to be free together, black and white.

Desmond Tutu, 1994

2

3

The anti-apartheid movement was an integral part of left-wing student life in the early 1980s. We checked labels when we shopped and never ever bought anything from South Africa. We protested outside branches of Barclays Bank (a major investor in South Africa) and danced to "Free Nelson Mandela" by The Specials at parties.

When Mandela was finally freed in February 1990, a huge multiracial crowd assembled in Trafalgar Square in London for a celebration rally and we sang "Free Nelson Mandela" with fists raised in the air in the black power salute.

Cath Senker, 2009

▶ A man at an ANC celebration rally in Soweto on Feb. 13, 1990, holds up a newspaper announcing Mandela's release. Mandela addressed the rally. In his speech, he thanked the members of the ANC, the South African Communist Party, the United Democratic Front, and "the working class of our country" for helping to end apartheid.

◀ A British author describes support for the anti-apartheid movement among university students in the United Kingdom in the 1980's.

4

NOW YOU KNOW

- In 1990, President Frederik Willem de Klerk ended the ban on the ANC and other anti-apartheid organizations.
- Nelson Mandela was a symbol for the anti-apartheid movement.
- Mandela was released from prison in February 1990.

Apartheid Abolished

THE GOVERNMENT REPEALED MOST OF THE REMAINING LAWS that had formed the legal basis of apartheid in 1990 and 1991. South Africa's many political groups made progress toward resolving their differences. They began to create a new political system in which all of the nation's racial groups would be fairly represented. In 1992, President F. W. de Klerk held a *referendum* (special vote) to ask white South Africans if they supported an end to apartheid and sharing power with the nation's black majority. Sixty-nine percent of the voters said yes. However, outbreaks of violence continued and threatened the peaceful process of change.

◀ The Afrikaner Resistance Movement, a group of white extremists, marches at a rally in support of apartheid in Pretoria in September 1989. Two men carry flags displaying the symbol of the Afrikaner Resistance Movement, three sevens in a white circle. The middle flag has a swastika, the symbol of Nazi Germany. The Afrikaner Resistance Movement wished to establish an independent state for Afrikaners alone.

▶ The Zulu leader Mangosuthu Buthelezi blames the ANC for violence in his 1990 book *South Africa: My Vision of the Future*. Buthelezi, the leader of the Inkatha Freedom Party, did not share the ANC's vision of a democratic government for the whole of South Africa. He hoped for the Zulu to retain power over their homeland, KwaZulu (now the province of KwaZulu-Natal) as a separate state.

Behaviour once encouraged by the ANC as integral to the struggle for liberation (it was all right and often a duty to murder "collaborators" and opponents, including town councillors, policemen, people like myself and anybody else targetted for assassination for whatever reason) is now reaping *anarchy* [lawlessness].

Violent youth, unemployed adults and others caught up in the chaos are out of control and even if the ANC does, at some stage, admit to regretting its militaristic stance, too much damage will already have been done. Smoke is in the air.

Mangosuthu Buthelezi, 1990

3

◀ The king of the Zulu, Goodwill Zwelithini (1948-), wearing dark glasses, rides in a parade in 1991 with Mangosuthu Buthelezi, his chief minister and uncle and the head of the Inkatha Freedom Party (IFP). In 1990 and 1991, the IFP fought the ANC for control of black townships around Johannesburg and in KwaZulu and Natal.

4

▶ The South African journalist Colin Legum (1919-2003) writes in 1993 about his fears for the future of his country in his newspaper feature service *Third World Reports*. During the early 1990's, South Africa struggled to achieve a peaceful change to democratic government. Many observers thought the country would descend into greater violence.

The four months from the beginning of the election campaign in January to voting day on 27th April, 1994, are likely to be horrendous: a time of political violence, of widespread intimidation [threatening people], possibly even a white-led rebellion, and acute hostility between the white-led parties, as well as between the predominantly [mainly] black-led parties.

Colin Legum, 1993

NOW YOU KNOW

• South Africa repealed most of the apartheid laws in 1990 and 1991.

• A majority of white South Africans supported efforts to end apartheid.

• Outbreaks of violence between the ANC and the IFP threatened the peaceful process of change.

The ANC Victory

I N 1993, SOUTH AFRICA EXTENDED VOTING RIGHTS TO PEOPLE OF ALL RACES. In 1994, the country held its first elections open to all races. The ANC won a majority of seats in the new National Assembly, and the Assembly elected Nelson Mandela president. The country's white leaders handed over power to South Africa's first multiracial government. South Africa resumed full participation in the United Nations (UN) and other international bodies. In 1995, South Africa hosted the Rugby World Cup for the first time as a democratic nation—and won.

1

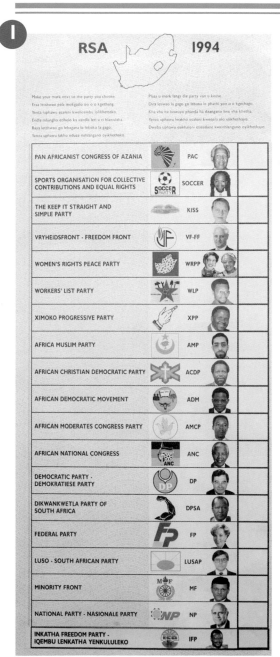

◄ The paper ballot for the 1994 election shows the name, symbol, and leader of each party. The bottom entry, the Inkatha Freedom Party, has a different format. Inkatha agreed to participate just one week before the election, and election officials added the party to the ballot at the last minute.

2

We stand here today as nothing more than a representative of the millions of our people who dared to rise up against a social system whose very essence is war, violence, racism, oppression, repression and the impoverishment of an entire people.

I am also here today as a representative of the millions of people across the globe, the anti-apartheid movement, the governments and organisations that joined with us, not to fight against South Africa as a country or any of its peoples, but to oppose an inhuman system and sue for a speedy end to the apartheid crime against humanity.

Nelson Mandela, Nobel Peace Prize acceptance speech, 1993

▲ In his Nobel Prize acceptance speech, Nelson Mandela gives credit to all the people in South Africa and around the world for their role in the anti-apartheid movement. Mandela and F. W. de Klerk shared the 1993 Nobel Peace Prize for their efforts to end apartheid.

▲ Voters stand in a long line at dawn in April 1994 at a polling station near Pretoria, waiting to vote in the country's first all-race elections. The ANC won 63 percent of the vote, the National Party received 20 percent, and the IFP got 11 percent.

▶ In a TV interview in 2003, South African rugby captain Francois Pienaar (1967-) recalls the excitement of winning the 1995 Rugby World Cup. Pienaar led the South African national team, the Springboks, to victory against the New Zealand All Blacks. After the match, President Mandela presented him with the cup.

It was just unbelievable on the streets of South Africa. For the first time all the people had come together and all races and religions were hugging each other. It was just wonderful . . .

Nelson Mandela said "thank you very much for what you've done for South Africa" but I said "thank you for what you've done."

I almost felt like hugging him but it wasn't appropriate, I guess.

Then I lifted the trophy which was unbelievable. I can't describe the feeling as I wouldn't do it justice.

Francois Pienaar, 2003

NOW YOU KNOW

- Nelson Mandela and F. W. de Klerk won the Nobel Peace Prize for efforts to end apartheid.
- The ANC won South Africa's first multiracial elections in April 1994, and Mandela became the country's president.
- South Africa resumed full participation in the UN and other international organizations.

The Truth Commission

To promote unity among South Africa's peoples, the new government established the Truth and Reconciliation Commission (TRC) in 1995. The TRC's task was to hear evidence about possible abuse of human rights during the apartheid era. The commission also aimed to discover the fate of missing persons who may have been the victims of kidnapping and murder. It began its work in 1996 and issued its final report in 2003. The TRC reported that the apartheid government had committed "gross violations of human rights." The commission, chaired by Desmond Tutu, also criticized anti-apartheid groups for their use of violence.

1

God has given us a great gift, ubuntu . . . ubuntu says I am human only because you are human. If I undermine your humanity, I dehumanise myself. You must do what you can to maintain this great harmony, which is perpetually undermined by resentment, anger, desire for vengeance. That's why African *jurisprudence* [legal theory] is *restorative* [repairing] rather than *retributive* [punishing].

Desmond Tutu, 1996

◀ In a 1996 newspaper interview, Desmond Tutu explains the African idea of *ubuntu* (mutual humanity). He argues that a legal system should seek to restore justice rather than to hand out punishment. Tutu, winner of the 1984 Nobel Peace Prize, chaired the Truth and Reconciliation Commission.

▶ Bernard Ngoepe (1947-   ), a South African judge, describes his frustration at the lack of punishment for crimes uncovered by the Truth and Reconciliation Commission. Ngoepe served on the Amnesty Committee of the TRC. Because of the TRC's amnesty provisions, many people who committed serious crimes went unpunished.

2

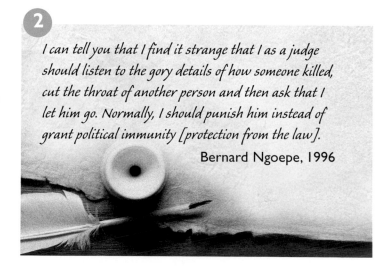

I can tell you that I find it strange that I as a judge should listen to the gory details of how someone killed, cut the throat of another person and then ask that I let him go. Normally, I should punish him instead of grant political immunity [protection from the law].

Bernard Ngoepe, 1996

③

▲ Gary Kruser, a government security officer, gives evidence at the TRC hearings in 1997. Kruser was arrested when he was an ANC member in the late 1980's. He describes how a policeman tortured him by pinning his arms to bars above his head. The TRC hearings revealed many acts of brutality by the police, security forces, and other agents of the white minority government.

NOW YOU KNOW

- The Truth and Reconciliation Commission revealed information about violent crimes committed under apartheid.

- The TRC helped discover what had happened to many missing persons.

- Some people criticized the TRC because it allowed criminal acts to go unpunished.

The Rainbow Nation

AFTER APARTHEID, SOUTH AFRICA BECAME KNOWN AS THE "RAINBOW NATION" because it included people of different colors. The government now represented the entire population. Jobs in government services were open to all races. However, white people generally remained better off than black people. The government attempted to improve the economic situation of black South Africans, with limited success. The country had social problems, too. Crime levels were high. The AIDS epidemic became a major problem. By 2000, more than 10 percent of South Africa's population was infected with HIV, the virus that causes AIDS. Large numbers of people suffered and died from AIDS.

1

On the day of the inauguration, I was overwhelmed with a sense of history. In the first decade of the twentieth century... the white-skinned peoples of South Africa patched up their differences and erected a system of racial domination against the dark-skinned peoples of their own land. The structure they created formed the basis of one of the harshest, most inhumane, societies the world has ever known. Now, in the last decade of the twentieth century, and my own eighth decade as a man, that system had been overturned forever and replaced by one that recognized the rights and freedoms of all peoples regardless of the color of their skin.

Nelson Mandela, 1994

▲ Nelson Mandela recalls in *Long Walk to Freedom* how he looked back with pride at the achievements of the anti-apartheid movement on the day that he took office as president of South Africa.

▶ A Zulu boy helps his white classmates learn isiZulu, the language of the Zulu people, in 1998. South Africa has 11 official languages, including English, Afrikaans, isiXhosa, and isiZulu.

▶ Laura de Lange, a 16-year-old student and a member of the Global Call to Action Against Poverty, describes the poverty she saw every day in Pretoria in 2006. In the first decade of the 2000's, South Africa had a 21 percent unemployment rate, and an estimated 50 percent of the population lived in poverty.

3

When I climb into my parents' car and drive to school, when I walk to the nearest coffee shop with my friends, when I do community outreach work—I see people living in the pieces of open ground where the wealthy developers have not built yet.

I see their houses made from plastic and rubbish. I hear their soft talking or animated voices as they wait for their turn to get soup from the big can. I feel their rough hands as I hand over the plastic cup filled with soup that probably means they will live a little longer.

Laura de Lange, 2006

4

◀ Residents walk through Kliptown, a part of Soweto, in 2005. A monument to the Freedom Charter was dedicated in Kliptown that year to mark the 50th anniversary of the charter's adoption in 1955. However, for many people in Kliptown, daily life has changed little since the 1950's.

NOW YOU KNOW

- After apartheid, the government represented all the people of South Africa.
- South Africa became known as the "rainbow nation" because it had people of different colors.
- A gap remained between the wealth of most white people and that of most black people.

Timeline

1880-1881	The Transvaal Boers defeat the British in the first Anglo-Boer War (also called the Anglo-Transvaal War).
1899-1902	The United Kingdom defeats the Boers in the second Anglo-Boer War (also called the Boer War or South African War). The two Boer republics become British colonies.
May 31, 1910	Cape Colony, Natal, the Orange Free State, and the Transvaal unite to form the Union of South Africa.
Jan. 8, 1912	Black South Africans found the South African Native National Congress (SANNC), a forerunner of the African National Congress (ANC), to fight for justice.
1913	The Natives' Lands Act sets aside land where blacks are allowed to settle.
1914	The Boer leader J. B. M. Hertzog founds the National Party to promote Afrikaner interests.
1944	The African National Congress forms the ANC Youth League for young people.
August 1946	Gold miners go on strike for about a week, demanding higher wages. The police crush the strike.
May 26, 1948	The National Party comes to power and begins to introduce apartheid laws. The party governs South Africa until 1994.
April 6, 1952	The ANC and the South African Indian Congress launch the Defiance Campaign Against Unjust Laws to refuse to obey apartheid rules.
1953	The Bantu Education Act brings most educational institutions under government control.
June 26, 1955	The Congress of the People in Kliptown, near Johannesburg, adopts the Freedom Charter.
1956	The South African government extends the pass laws to nonwhite women.
1956-1961	Nelson Mandela and other anti-apartheid leaders stand trial on charges of treason. The judge finds them not guilty.
1959	ANC leader Robert Mangaliso Sobukwe leaves the organization to form the Pan Africanist Congress.
March 21, 1960	The police kill 69 black demonstrators in what becomes known as the Sharpeville Massacre.
1961	The ANC forms a military wing called Umkhonto we Sizwe, which launches a campaign of sabotage.
May 31, 1961	South Africa becomes a republic.
June 12, 1964	Several ANC leaders, including Nelson Mandela, are sentenced to life imprisonment.
1964	The International Olympic Committee bans South Africa from the Olympic Games.
Late 1960's	The South African government begins to force blacks to move to separate areas called homelands or bantustans. The bantustans are abolished in 1994.
1975	Mangosuthu Buthelezi sets up the Inkatha Freedom Party.
June 16, 1976	During the Soweto Uprising, the police kill two black children.
Aug. 20, 1983	A broad-based alliance of anti-apartheid groups forms the United Democratic Front (UDF).
Sept. 3, 1984	The government introduces a new constitution that offers some rights to Coloured and Asian people.
1985	The Congress of South African Trade Unions (COSATU) is founded.
1985	Waves of strikes and protests take place across South Africa.
June 12, 1986	The South African government declares a nationwide state of emergency.
Feb. 2, 1990	President F. W. de Klerk ends the ban on the ANC, the Pan Africanist Congress, the South African Communist Party, and other anti-apartheid organizations.
Feb. 11, 1990	Nelson Mandela is released from prison.
1990-1991	De Klerk's government repeals most of the apartheid laws.
Oct. 15, 1993	Mandela and de Klerk jointly receive the Nobel Peace Prize.
April 27, 1994	The ANC wins South Africa's first multiracial elections. Mandela becomes president of the country.
1995	The government establishes the Truth and Reconciliation Commission (TRC). The commission begins its work in 1996 and issues its final report in 2003.

Sources

4-5 Document 2 – Phipson, Thomas. *Letters and Other Writings of a Natal Sheriff, Thomas Phipson, 1815-76*. Cape Town: Oxford Univ. Pr., 1968. Print. Document 4 – Luuli, Martin. Testimony before the South African Native Affairs Commission., 1904. Available in Karis, Thomas, and Gwendolen M. Carter, eds. *From Protest to Challenge: A Documentary History of African Politics in South Africa, 1882-1990*. Vol. 1. Stanford: Hoover, 1972. Print.

6-7 Document 1 – Hertzog, J. B. M. Quoted in Moodie, T. Dunbar. *The Rise of Afrikanerdom*. Berkeley: Univ. of Calif. Pr., 1975. Print. Document 3 – Plaatje, Sol T. *Native Life in South Africa, Before and Since the European War and the Boer Rebellion*. London: P. S. King, 1916. Print.

8-9 Document 1 – African National Congress. African Bill of Rights. Art. 5, 1923. Available in *The ANC and the Bill of Rights, 1923 to 1993*. Johannesburg: ANC Dept. of Information and Publicity, 1994. Print. Document 4 – South Africa. *Kerk en Stad*. Stellenbosch: Pro Ecclesia-Boekhandel, 1947. Quoted in Grundlingh, Albert. "Afrikaner Nationalism in the 1930s and 1940s." *South African History Online*. SAHO, n.d. Web. 28 Apr. 2010.

10-11 Document 1 – African National Congress Youth League. ANC Youth League Basic Policy Document, 1948. *African National Congress*. Web. 28 Apr. 2010. Document 3 – Chamber of Mines. Quoted in Wilson, Francis. *Labour in the South African Gold Mines, 1911-1969*. Cambridge: Cambridge Univ. Pr., 1972. Print.

12-13 Document 1 – Eloff, G. *Rasse en Rasvermenging*. Bloemfontein: Nasionale Pers, 1942. Quoted in Thompson, Leonard. *A History of South Africa*. 3rd ed. New Haven: Yale Univ. Pr., 2001. Print. Document 3 – Union of South Africa. Population Registration Act No. 30 of 1950. Quoted in the *Truth and Reconciliation Commission of South Africa Report*. Vol. 1, Cape Town: Truth and Reconciliation Commission, 1998. Print.

14-15 Document 2 – Natal Indian Congress. *Natal Indian Congress Provincial Conference Agenda Book*. 21-23 Nov. 1958. Print. Document 3 – Sindane, Lucky. "Sophiatown: Recalling the Loss." *South-Africa.info*. Big Media Publishers, 10 Feb. 2005. Web. 29 Apr. 2010.

16-17 Document 1 – Verwoerd, Hendrik. Speech to Parliament about Bantu education. 7 June 1954. Quoted in "Bantu Education." *South Africa: Overcoming Apartheid, Building Democracy*. Michigan State Univ. n.d. Web. 29 Apr. 2010. Document 2 – Matthews, Z. K. and Monica H. Wilson. *Freedom for My People: The Autobiography of Z. K. Matthews*. London: R. Collings, 1981. Print.

18-19 Document 1 – Aucamp, M. Letter to the African National Congress. 29 Jan. 1952. *African National Congress*. Web. 29 Apr. 2010. Document 3 – Ngoyi, Lilian.

20-21 Document 1 – African National Congress. The Freedom Charter. 26 June 1955. *South African History Online*. Web. 29 Apr. 2010. Document 4 – Rumpff, F. L. H. Quoted in "The Treason Trial: 1956-1961." *South African History Online*. SAHO, n.d. Web. 29 Apr. 2010.

22-23 Document 2 – Sisulu, Albertina. Document 4 – Unnamed South African journalist. Interview. 1980.

24-25 Document 1– Anthem of the Pan Africanist Congress. 1960. Quoted in Sampson, Anthony. *Mandela: The Authorized Biography*. New York: Knopf, 1999. Document 2 – Mandela, Nelson. *Long Walk to Freedom: The Autobiography of Nelson Mandela*. New York: Little, Brown & Co., 1994. Print.

26-27 Document 3 – "Police Fire Kills 63 Africans." *Guardian* 22 Mar. 1960: n. pag. Guardian.co.uk. Web. 29 Apr. 2010. Document 4 – Mandela, Nelson. *Long Walk to Freedom*. New York: Little, Brown & Co., 1994. Print.

28-29 Document 2 – Umkhonto we Sizwe. Manifesto of Umkhonto we Sizwe. 16 Dec. 1961. *O'Malley–The Heart of Hope*. Web. 29 Apr. 2010. Document 4 – South Africa. General Law Amendment [Sabotage] Act, No. 76 of 1962. Quoted in the *Truth and Reconciliation Commission of South Africa Report*. Vol. 1. Cape Town: Truth and Reconciliation Commission, 1998. Print.

30-31 Document 2 – Brand, Christo. Interview by John Carlin.

Frontline. PBS, 25 May 1995. Web. 4 May 2010. Document 4 – Mandela, Nelson. Letter to General J. C. Steyn. 1970. Quoted in Sampson, Anthony. *Mandela*. New York: Knopf, 1999.

32-33 Document 1 – South Africa. Department of Bantu Administration and Development. General Circular No. 25, 1967. Quoted in Bernstein, Hilda. *For Their Triumphs and for Their Tears. Women in Apartheid South Africa*. London: International Defence and Aid Fund for Southern Africa, 1985. South African History Online. Web. 30 Apr. 2010. Document 2 – Unnamed Mfengu woman. Interview. 1983.

34-35 Document 1 – Serote, Mongane Wally. "City Johannesburg." *Yakhal'inkomo*. Johannesburg: Renoster Books, 1972. Print. Document 2 – La Guma, Alex. "Apartheid and the Coloured People of South Africa." 1972. *African National Congress*. Web. 30 Apr. 2010.

36-37 Document 1 – McGregor, Peter J. Interview by James Middleton. 1993. *Green Left Weekly* 7 Dec. 2005: n. pag. Web. 30 Apr. 2010. Document 4 – Black Leadership Conference on Southern Africa. African-American Manifesto on Southern Africa. 1976.

38-39 Document 1 – Biko, Steve, and Aelred Stubbs, ed. *I Write What I Like*. London: Bowerdean Pr., 1978. Print. Document 3 – Kane-Berman, John Stuart. *Soweto: Black Revolt, White Reaction*. Johannesburg: Ravan Pr., 1978. Print.

40-41 Document 1 – Huddleston, Trevor. *Father Huddleston's Picture Book*. London: Kliptown Books, 1990. Print. *African National Congress*. Web. 30 Apr. 2010. Document 2 – Gordimer, Nadine. *The Lying Days*. London: Gollancz, 1953. Print.

42-43 Document 1 – Stals, E. L. P. "Geskiedenis van die Afrikaner-Broederbond, 1918-1994." MS. 1998. Quoted in Giliomee, Hermann B. *The Afrikaners*. Charlottesville: Univ. of Virginia Pr., 2003. Print. Document 3 – Unnamed mineworker. Quoted in Chipkin, Ivor. "Nationalism As Such: Violence During South Africa's Political Transition." *Public Culture* 16.2 (2004): 315-35. Print.

44-45 Document 2 – United Democratic Front, 1987. Quoted in Houston, Gregory F. *The National Liberation Struggle in South Africa*. Farnham: Ashgate. Print. Document 4 – Steinbreder, H. John and John Nielsen, ed. "Circling the Wagons in South Africa." *Fortune*, 7 July 1986: n.pag. *CNNMoney.com*. Web. 4 May 2010.

46-47 Document 2 – Leach, Graham. *South Africa: No Easy Path to Peace*. Boston: Routledge & Kegan Paul, 1986. Print. Document 4 – Sparks, Allister. "Angolan Forces Fall Back from Site of Heavy Battle." *The Washington Post* 9 Oct. 1985: A1+. Microfilm.

48-49 Document 2 – Rupert, Anton. Letter to P.W. Botha. Jan. 1986. Quoted in Krog, Antjie. *Country of My Skull: Guilt, Sorrow, and the Limits of Forgiveness in the New South Africa*. New York: Three Rivers Pr., 2000. Print. Document 3 – Inkatha Freedom Party, about 1987.

50-51 Document 1 – Tutu, Desmond, and John Allen ed. *The Rainbow People of God*. New York: Doubleday, 1994. Print. Document 3 – Cath Senker, personal recollection, 2009.

52-53 Document 2 – Buthelezi, Mangosuthu G. *South Africa: My Vision of the Future*. New York: St. Martin's Pr., 1990. Print. Document 4 – Legum, Colin. Third World Reports. 24 Nov. 1993. Quoted in Spence, J. E. *Change in South Africa*. New York: Council on Foreign Relations Pr., 1994. Print.

54-55 Document 2 – Mandela, Nelson. Nobel Lecture. 10 Dec. 1993. Nobelprize.org. Web. 3 May 2010. Document 4 – Pienaar, Francois. Pienaar, Francois. Interview by Matt Majendie. *BBC Sport*. BBC, 24 Sept. 2003. Web. 3 May 2010.

56-57 Document 1 – Tutu, Desmond. Interview. *Mail & Guardian*. 17 Mar. 1996. Quoted in Brudholm, Thomas. *Resentment's Virtue: Jean Améry and the Refusal to Forgive*. Philadelphia : Temple Univ. Pr., 2008. Print. Document 2 – Ngoepe, Bernard. Personal interview by Richard A. Wilson. 1996.

58-59 Document 1 – Mandela, Nelson. *Long Walk to Freedom*. New York: Little, Brown & Co., 1994. Print. Document 3 – De Lange, Laura. Interview by Moyiga Nduru. "The Reality of Poverty Is Everywhere." Inter Press Service News Agency. 16 Oct. 2006.

Additional Resources

Books

Apartheid In South Africa (Witness to History series) by David Downing. San Val, 2005

Apartheid in South Africa by Michael J. Martin, Lucent Books, 2006

Desmond Tutu by Samuel Willard Crompton. Chelsea House Publications, 2006

The End of Apartheid in South Africa by Liz Sonneborn. Chelsea House Publications, 2010

The Fall of Apartheid in South Africa (Monumental Milestones: Great Events of Modern Times series) by Melissa Koosman. Mitchell Lane Publishers, 2009

The Making of Modern South Africa: Conquest, Apartheid, Democracy by Nigel Worden. Wiley-Blackwell, 2007

Nelson Mandela by Lenny Hort and Laaren Brown. DK Children, 2006

Playing the Enemy: Nelson Mandela and the Game That Made a Nation by John Carlin. Penguin Press HC, 2008

South Africa: The Rise and Fall of Apartheid by Nancy L. Clark and William H. Worger. Longman, 2004

Tree Shaker: The Story of Nelson Mandela by Bill Keller. Kingfisher, 2008

Websites

http://www.anc.org.za/ancdocs/history/
The Historical Documents section of the African National Congress (ANC) site includes many documents produced by the ANC during its struggle against apartheid.

http://www.unmultimedia.org/photo/gallery.jsp?mode=auto&query=subject%3AApartheid
A United Nations site displays photos of the apartheid era.

http://www.info.gov.za/aboutsa/history.htm#Apartheid
A South African Government Information site provides information about the apartheid policy, the end of apartheid, and the new era of freedom in South Africa.

Index

Index

Acknowledgments

AKG-Images: 4 (North Wind Picture Archives), 20, 23, 26, 28, 29, 31, 38, 55 (African Pictures); **AP:** 19 (Jurgen Schadeberg), 39, 52 (Topham); **Avusa Media Ltd:** 48; **Corbis:** 17 (© Alain Nogues/Sygma), 43 (© Patrick Durand/Sygma), 44 (© Reuters), 49, 50 (© David Turnley), 53 (© Reuters), 54 (© Michael Nicholson), 58 (© Ed Kashi), 59 (© Jon Hrusa/epa); **Getty:** Cover, 9, 10 (UPPA/Photoshot), 12, 18, 22, 26, 33 (Time Life Pictures), 35, 37 (Popperfoto), 41, 45, 47 (Time Life Pictures), 46 (Redferns), 51 (AFP); **Mayibuye©Link:** 30; **Sipa Press/Rex Features:** 21, 36; **Topfoto:** 5 (Roger-Viollet/Top), 6 , 8 (Print Collector/HIP), 11, 13, 57 (Image Works); **United Nations:** 14, **University of the Witwatersrand, Johannesburg:** 7 (William Cullen Library), 25.

Cover main image: **Corbis** (Reuters); inset image: **Getty Images** (Time & Life Pictures)